D0409258

KEEP CALM
AND
GET A CAT

Susan McMullan

BLACK & WHITE PUBLISHING

First published 2013
by Black & White Publishing Ltd
29 Ocean Drive, Edinburgh EH6 6JL

1 3 5 7 9 10 8 6 4 2   13 14 15 16

ISBN: 978 1 84502 650 9

Design by Stuart Polson
Typeset by RefineCatch Limited, Bungay, Suffolk
Printed and bound in Poland
www.hussarbooks.pl

CONTENTS

PROVERBS

You will always be lucky if you know how to make friends with strange cats.
Colonial American proverb

After dark all cats are leopards.
Native American proverb

If you stared deep into a cat's
eyes you would be able to see
into the world of spirits.

English proverb

It is better to feed one cat
than many mice.

Norwegian proverb

In a cat's eye, all things belong to cats.
English proverb

A rose has thorns, a cat has claws;
certainly both are worth the risk.
Anonymous

Beware of people who dislike cats.
Irish proverb

It is better to be a mouse in a cat's mouth than a man in a lawyer's hands.
Spanish proverb

Happy owner, happy cat.
Indifferent owner, reclusive cat.
Chinese proverb

A cat has nine lives. For three he
plays, for three he strays, and
for the last three he stays.
English proverb

Happy is the home with
at least one cat.
Italian proverb

The cat was created when
the lion sneezed.
Arabian proverb

Curiosity killed the cat
but satisfaction brought it back!
English proverb

I gave an order to a cat,
and the cat gave it to its tail.
Chinese proverb

The cat loves fish but hates wet feet.
Medieval proverb

Those who dislike cats
will be carried to the
cemetery in the rain.
Dutch proverb

The dog may be wonderful prose,
but only the cat is poetry.

French proverb

A cat is a lion in a jungle
of small bushes.

Indian proverb

If stretching were wealth,
the cat would be rich.

African proverb

An overdressed woman is
like a cat dressed in saffron.

Egyptian proverb

Handsome cats and fat dung heaps
are the sign of a good farmer.

French proverb

When the cat and mouse agree,
the grocer is ruined.

Persian proverb

A cat may look at a king.
Anonymous

An old cat will not learn
how to dance.
Moroccan proverb

Cats, flies and women are
ever at their toilets.

French proverb

The cat who frightens the
mice away is as good as
the cat who eats them.

German proverb

A cat bitten once by a snake
dreads even rope.

Arabic proverb

When rats infest the Palace,
a lame cat is better than
the swiftest horse.

Chinese proverb

A cat may go to a monastery,
but she still remains a cat.
Ethiopian proverb

SAYINGS

Cat's motto: No matter what
you've done wrong, always try to
make it look like the dog did it.

When the cat's away,
the mice will play.

Who would believe such pleasure
from a wee ball o' fur?

The cat that catches no mice
does not earn his keep.

Don't trust the weak appearance of the wolf or the disappearance of the cat: they'll both make a comeback.

A good cat deserves a good rat.

By scratching and biting cat
and dog come together.

It is a bold mouse that makes
her nest in the cat's ear.

All cats are grey in the dark.

He who plays with a cat must
bear its scratches.

Thousands of years ago, cats were worshipped as gods. Cats have never forgotten this.

When the cat and the calf play the fiddle, you are caught in the middle.

Keep an eye on the cat and
another on the frying pan.

A cat is mighty dignified
until the dog comes by.

The cat shuts his eyes while
he steals the cream.

The eye of the housewife
makes the cat fat.

The old cat refuses to admit that the
face in the looking glass is her own.

What joy fills the mouse when
the cat is out of the house?

Lions are not terrified of cats.

There are many ways to skin a cat.

The cat is honest when the
meat is out of her reach.

A cornered cat becomes
as fierce as a lion.

Touch not a cat but a glove.

If you don't feed the cats
you must feed the rats.

Wanton kittens make sober cats.

A cat sleeps fat, yet walks thin.

One cat just leads to another.
Ernest Hemingway

The cat has too much
spirit to have no heart.
Ernest Menaul

The city of cats and the city of men exist one inside the other, but they are not the same city.

Italo Calvino

When Mother Nature saw fit to remove the tail of the Manx, she left in place of the tail more cat.

Mary E. Stewart

A cat improves the garden
wall in sunshine and the
hearth in foul weather.

Judith Merkle Riley

SUPERSTITIONS

Dreaming of a white cat
means good luck.

If a cat washes behind
its ears, it will rain.

A strange black cat on your
porch brings prosperity.

A cat sneezing is a good omen
for everyone who hears it.

A cat sleeping with all four
paws tucked under means
cold weather ahead.

If you give your milk to the
cat you must drink water
out of the sink.

It is bad luck to see a
white cat at night.

Whenever the cat of the
house is black, the lasses of
lovers will have no lack.

When a weasel and a cat kiss,
the future is not very bright.

People that hate cats will come
back as mice in their next life.
Faith Resnick

When moving to a new home,
always put the cat through the
window instead of the door
so that it will not leave.

When you see a one-eyed cat, spit on your thumb, stamp it in the palm of your hand and make a wish. The wish will come true.

CATS AND PEOPLE

A cat sees no good reason why
it should obey another animal,
even if it does stand on two legs.
Sarah Thompson

Everything I know I learned from
my cat: When you're hungry, eat.
When you're tired, nap in a
sunbeam. When you go to
the vet's, pee on your owner.

Gary Smith

I have studied many
philosophers and many
cats. The wisdom of cats
is infinitely superior.

Hippolyte Taine

Cat people are different to
the extent that they generally
are not conformists. How
could they be with a cat
running their lives?

Louis J. Camuti

Cats do care. For example,
they know instinctively what
time we have to be at work
in the morning and they
wake us up twenty minutes
before the alarm goes off.

Michael Nelson

Women and cats will do as
they please, and men and
dogs should relax and get
used to the idea.

Robert A. Heinlein

With their qualities of cleanliness,
discretion, affection, patience,
dignity and courage, how many
of us, I ask you, would be
capable of becoming cats?

Fernand Mery

If man could be crossed with
the cat it would improve man,
but deteriorate the cat.

Mark Twain

After scolding one's cat one
looks into its face and is seized
by the ugly suspicion that it
understood every word.
And has filed it for reference.

Charlotte Gray

Cats are kindly masters,
just so long as you
remember your place.
Paul Gray

I love cats because I enjoy
my home, and little by little,
they become its visible soul.

Jean Cocteau

No amount of time can erase
the memory of a good cat,
and no amount of masking
tape can ever totally remove
his fur from your couch.

Leo Dworken

If we treated everyone we meet with the same affection we bestow upon our favourite cat, they, too, would purr.

Martin Buxbaum

Cats always know whether
people like or dislike them. They
do not always care enough
to do anything about it.

Winifred Carriere

If a cat does something, we call
it instinct; if we do the same
thing, for the same reason,
we call it intelligence.

Will Cuppy

There's no need for a
piece of sculpture in a
home that has a cat.

Wesley Bates

Cats' hearing apparatus is
built to allow the human
voice to easily go in one
ear and out the other.

Stephen Baker

As every cat owner knows,
nobody owns a cat.
Ellen Perry Berkeley

A cat has absolute emotional honesty: human beings, for one reason or another, may hide their feelings, but a cat does not.

Ernest Hemingway

In the beginning, God created
man, but seeing him so feeble,
He gave him the cat.

Warren Eckstein

There are few things in life
more heart-warming than
to be welcomed by a cat.

Tay Hohoff

Most beds sleep up to six cats.
Ten cats without the owner.

Stephen Baker

One reason we admire cats is for their proficiency in one-upmanship. They always seem to come out on top, no matter what they are doing, or pretend they do.

Barbara Webster

As anyone who has ever been around a cat for any length of time well knows, cats have enormous patience with the limitations of the human kind.

Cleveland Amory

If a cat did not put a firm paw
down now and then, how could
his human remain possessed?

Winifred Carriere

If you are worthy of its affection,
a cat will be your friend, but
never your slave.

Théophile Gautier

You can keep a dog; but it
is the cat who keeps people,
because cats find humans
useful domestic animals.

George Mikes

If you yell at a cat, you're the one
who is making a fool of yourself.

Unknown

It is remarkable, in cats, that
the outer life they reveal to
their masters is one of
perpetual boredom.

Robley Wilson, Jr

You can tell your cat anything
and he'll still love you. If you
lose your job or your best friend,
your cat will think no less of you.

Helen Powers

A cat can maintain a position of curled up somnolence on your knee until you are nearly upright. To the last minute she hopes your conscience will get the better of you and you will settle down again.

Pam Brown

The way to get on with a
cat is to treat it as an
equal – or even better,
as the superior it knows
itself to be.

Elizabeth Peters

Cats were put into the world to
disprove the dogma that all things
were created to serve man.

Paul Gray

There is, indeed, no single
quality of the cat that man
could not emulate to his
advantage.

Carl Van Vechten

What greater gift than
the love of a cat?

Charles Dickens

Do not meddle in the affairs
of cats, for they are subtle
and will pee on your computer.

Bruce Graham

People who love cats have some
of the biggest hearts around.

Susan Easterly

Everything comes to those
who wait . . . except a cat.
Unknown

My husband said it was
him or the cat . . . I miss
him sometimes.

Unknown

LIFE ACCORDING TO CATS

Cats can be cooperative when
something feels good, which,
to a cat, is the way everything
is supposed to feel as much
of the time as possible.

Roger Caras

If cats could talk, they wouldn't.
Nan Porter

Cats are connoisseurs of comfort.
James Herriot

Cats can work out mathematically
the exact place to sit that will
cause most inconvenience.

Pam Brown

A cat doesn't know what it
wants and wants more of it.

Richard Hexem

A cat's behaviour is a direct reflection of his feelings.

Carole Wilbourn

Cats aren't clean, they're just covered with cat spit.

John S. Nichols

There are two means of refuge from the miseries of life: music and cats.

Albert Schweitzer

Cats are creatures that express a multitude of moods and attitudes.

Karen Brademeyer

Cats seem to go on the principle
that it never does any harm to
ask for what you want.

Joseph Wood Krutch

A cat with kittens nearly
always decides sooner or
later to move them.

Sidney Denham

More than likely it was the
cat who first coined and put
into practice the sage advice:
If you would have a thing done
well, you must do it yourself.

Lawrence N. Johnson

The cat has always been
associated with the moon.
Like the moon it comes to life
at night, escaping from humanity
and wandering over housetops
with its eyes beaming out
through the darkness.

Patricia Dale-Green

A cat determined not to be found can fold itself up like a pocket handkerchief if it wants to.

Louis J. Camuti

Are cats lazy? Well, more power to them if they are. Which one of us has not entertained the dream of doing just as he likes, when and how he likes, and as much as he likes?

Fernand Mery

A cat is a puzzle for which
there is no solution.
Hazel Nicholson

A cat is never vulgar.
Carl Van Vechten

A cat isn't fussy – just so long as you remember he likes his milk in the shallow, rose-patterned saucer and his fish on the blue plate. From which he will take it, and eat it off the floor.

Arthur Bridges

Some people say that cats are sneaky, evil and cruel. True, and they have many other fine qualities as well.

Missy Dizick

When addressed, a gentleman
cat does not move a muscle.
He looks as if he hasn't heard.
Mary Sarton

Prowling his own quiet backyard
or asleep by the fire, he is still only
a whisker away from the wilds.

Jean Burden

Cats are intended to teach us that not everything in nature has a purpose.

Garrison Keillor

A cat can purr its way
out of anything.
Donna McCrohan

The trouble with cats is that
they've got no tact.
P.G. Wodehouse

The cat is, above all things,
a dramatist.
Margaret Benson

The ideal of calm exists
in a sitting cat.
Jules Renard

Cats are the ultimate narcissists. You can tell this by all the time they spend on personal grooming. Dogs aren't like this. A dog's idea of personal grooming is to roll on a dead fish.

James Gorman

Way down deep, we're all
motivated by the same urges.
Cats have the courage to
live by them.

Jim Davis

A meow massages the heart.
Stuart McMillan

I believe cats to be spirits come to
earth. A cat, I am sure, could walk on
a cloud without coming through.
Jules Verne

You cannot look at a sleeping
cat and feel tense.

Jane Pauley

There is no snooze button on
a cat who wants breakfast.

Unknown

Most cats, when they are out want to be in, and vice versa, and often simultaneously.

Louis F. Camuti

The phrase 'domestic cat' is an oxymoron.

George F. Will

Civilisation is defined by
the presence of cats.

Unknown

Time spent with cats
is never wasted.

May Sarton

One small cat changes coming home
to an empty house to coming home.

Pam Brown

Cats like doors left open in
case they change their minds.

Rosemary Nisbet

There are people who reshape
the world by force or argument,
but the cat just lies there,
dozing, and the world quietly
reshapes itself to suit his
comfort and convenience.

Allen and Ivy Dodd

A cat allows you to sleep
on the bed. On the edge.

Jenny de Vries

It's really the cat's house —
we just pay the mortgage.

Unknown

The cat seldom interferes
with other people's rights.
His intelligence keeps him
from doing many of the foolish
things that complicate life.
Carl Van Vechten

In reality, cats are probably
better off remaining indoors
and sending out their humans to
deal with the outside world.

Dr Phyllis Sherman Raschke

The man who carries a cat by
the tail learns something he can
learn in no other way.
Mark Twain

He has become a much better cat than I have a person. With his gentle urgings, he made me realise that life doesn't end just because one has a few obstacles to overcome.

Mary F. Graf

A cat will do what it wants
when it wants, and there's not
a thing you can do about it.
Frank Perkins

Cats are a mysterious kind of folk. There is more passing in their minds than we are aware of.

Sir Walter Scott

Cats are a tonic, they are a laugh,
they are a cuddle, they are at least
pretty just about all of the time
and beautiful some of the time.

Roger Caras

Even overweight cats instinctively
know the cardinal rule: when fat,
arrange yourself in slim poses.

John Weitz

I wish I could write as
mysterious as a cat.
Edgar Allan Poe

Who among us hasn't envied a cat's
ability to ignore the cares of daily life
and to relax completely?

Karen Brademeyer

CATS AND
OTHER ANIMALS

No matter how much cats fight, there always seems to be plenty of kittens.

Abraham Lincoln

Of all God's creatures, there is only
one that cannot be made the slave
of the lash. That one is the cat.

Mark Twain

Dogs come when they're called;
cats take a message and get
back to you later.

Mary Bly

I like pigs. Dogs look up to us.
Cats look down on us. Pigs
treat us as equals.
Sir Winston Churchill

There is no more intrepid
explorer than a kitten.

Jules Champfleury

A dog will flatter you but you
have to flatter the cat.

George Mikes

If a dog jumps into your lap
it is because he is fond of you;
but if a cat does the same
thing it is because your
lap is warmer.

A.N. Whitehead

Intelligence in the cat is underrated.
Louis Wain

The smallest feline is a masterpiece.
Leonardo da Vinci

If animals could speak, the dog
would be a blundering outspoken
fellow; but the cat would have
the rare grace of never saying
a word too much.

Mark Twain

Cats are smarter than dogs.
You can't get eight cats to
pull a sled through snow.

Jeff Valdez

Even the stupidest cat seems
to know more than any dog.

Eleanor Clark

Winners are different. They're
a different breed of cat.

Byron Nelson

Of all animals, the cat alone attains to the contemplative life. He regards the wheel of existence from without, like the Buddha.

Andrew Lang

Of all domestic animals, the cat
is the most expressive. His face
is capable of showing a wide
range of expressions. His tail
is a mirror of his mind. His
gracefulness is surpassed only
by his agility. And, along with
all these, he has a sense of humour.

Walter Chandoha

A dog is like a liberal: he
wants to please everybody.
A cat doesn't really need to
know that everybody loves him.

William Kunstler

The reason cats climb is so
that they can look down on
almost every other animal . . . it's
also the reason they hate birds.

KC Buffington

Dogs eat. Cats dine.
Ann Taylor

There is no such thing as 'just a cat'.
Robert A. Heinlein

The cat has been described as the most perfect animal, the acme of muscular perfection and the supreme example in the animal kingdom of the coordination of mind and muscle.

Roseanne Ambrose Brown

Cats are successful underachievers.
They only need to purr in order
to get free food and TLC. What
other creature can lay around
the house doing nothing beyond
purring, and still get free food
and TLC?

Jim Aites

A cat is nobody's fool.
Heywood Brown

The domestic cat seems to
have greater confidence in
itself than in anyone else.
Lawrence N. Johnson

Cats look beyond appearances –
beyond species entirely, it seems –
to peer into the heart.

Barbara L. Diamond

Some animals are secretive;
some are shy. A cat is private.
Leonard Michaels

Among animals, cats are the top-hatted, frock-coated statesmen going about their affairs at their own pace.

Robert Sterns

There are many intelligent
species in the universe. They
are all owned by cats.

Anonymous

Dogs believe they are human.
Cats believe they are God.

Jeff Valdez

Nothing's more playful than
a young cat, nor more grave
than an old one.

Thomas Fuller

Every dog has his day – but the
nights are reserved for the cats.
Unknown

In the middle of a world that
had always been a bit mad,
the cat walks with confidence.

Rose F. Kennedy

A cat is the only domestic animal I
know who toilet trains itself and does
a damned impressive job of it.

Joseph Epstein

A cat is a tiger that is
fed by hand.

Vakaoka Genrin

There are many intelligent
species in the universe.
They are all owned by cats.

Anonymous